COBRA

Y0-CAA-419

Osprey Colour Series

COBRA

BEKI ADAM

Contents

Published in 1989 by Osprey Publishing Limited
59 Grosvenor Street, London WIX 9DA

© Beki Adam 1989

This book is copyrighted under the Berne Con-
vention. All rights reserved. Apart from any fair
dealing for the purpose of private study,
research, criticism or review, as permitted
under the Copyright Act, 1956, no part of this
publication may be reproduced, stored in a
retrieval system, or transmitted in any form or
by any means, electronic, electrical, chemical,
mechanical, optical, photocopying, recording or
otherwise, without prior written permission. All
enquiries should be addressed to the publisher.

British Library Cataloguing in Publication Data
Adam, Beki

   Cobra.— (Osprey colour series)
   I. Cobra racing sports cars. AC to 1989
   I. Title
   796.7'2
ISBN 0-85045-809-9

Editor Nicholas Collins
Art direction Martin Richards
Designer Paul Kime

Printed in Hong Kong

Acknowledgements

Writing this book has been lots of fun, but it would never have happened without the men and women who willingly gave of their time and photographs to
help me. To all of them I extend my sincerest thanks. I do not like to single out
individuals, but feel I must mention Andrew Morland for his skill with a camera.
Some of the best material, including the section on Autokraft and building the
Mk IV, is his.

Introduction

The Cobra was a car that came about quickly, stayed for a short while, and disappeared just as quickly, almost always in a cloud of dust. To write a book full of intricate detail and carefully traced histories is an unrealistic reflection of the car. It was created in a time when automotive initiaters did not involve themselves with trivialities.

Yes it's another Cobra book. There are, let's face it, a lot, which says something for the Cobra – the book market it has created seems insatiable. The trouble is, that, with few exceptions, each book holds its own banner. Many choose to specialize in either the production or racing history. Others, in dealing with a partnership that spanned the Atlantic, and, naturally being written on one side or another, seem to result in a heavy bias according to which side of the water the author types on. Admittedly the US seemed, at the end of the 1960s, to have taken more credit than they deserved for the Cobra's success, but does it really matter?

The trouble with writing a book twenty years later is not fading memories so much as fading patience. As Carroll Shelby, or Brian Angliss, now joint owner of AC, (and sole owner of Autokraft), will explain, once you have told the story a few dozen times, it gets boring. The temptation to exaggerate, to add more variety, interest, or whatever is irresistible. Turning to the books, articles, road tests, and racing results of the time poses another problem – basic facts and figures differed dramatically, the temptation was obviously too great even then.

All I have attempted to do is to illustrate the story of the AC

Above
More at home in sunnier climes, the 289 Roadster basks in Californian sunshine

6

Cobra. How it came about, what it did then, and, just as importantly, what it's doing now. For let's not forget that the Cobra still stirs, waiting to strike. The only difference is now it lies under the shadow of the crumbling Brooklands banking. Having been warned of the pitfalls, and not wanting to write a book full of fiction posing as fact, I've decided to leave out the more unfounded amusing little anecdotes. You can find them, if you must, in other works.

The Cobra story is shrouded in a certain amount of mystery. Arguments still simmer, even today, about who should take the credit for this or that. I do not intend to ignore them completely (it's irresistible in a position with no direct comeback not to add your own opinion) but, having mentioned them in passing, I will take up no more of your time, my space, or my publisher's paper. Having ascertained that many facts are in fact, fabrications, it seems a fairly futile exercise. I'm not even sure such details really matter – the most important thing is that the car was built in the first place. Also, I feel that an in-depth study of who-really-in-the-very-first-instance-came-up-with-the-very-first-idea-for-such-and-such-a-design will, if you take the research far enough, lead you back to the beginning of the motor car.

My concern is the Cobra story, the complete story, and this book, concise though it might be, is an attempt to relay just that. It's never been written before. It could not have been – the Cobra story has only just come, in 1989, full circle, with the ends, as you will discover, very neatly tied up.

Following pages
Vin Davison's Tojeiro Special with a brand new set of wheels, and a brand new registration – it's now an AC Ace

The Cobra Story

In 1923 a few entrepreneurial, even eccentric, speed mad Britons were 'building' their own cars, which came to be known as 'specials'. Also, a small, almost archaic automotive company based in Thames Ditton, by the name of Autocarriers Ltd, were, under the jurisdiction of a certain S F Edge, starting an involvement with motor racing. A couple in Leesbury, East Texas were celebrating the arrival of a son, born 11 January, and given the name Carroll Shelby, and a huge automobile manufacturer in America, The Ford Motor Company, had just seen its 4,000,000th engine come down the production line. In 1923, no one could ever have guessed that these four events, all happening in quite different places around the world, would somehow later be interlinked and irrevocably interwoven, resulting in the manufacture of one of the world's most renowned, remarkable, and remembered racing sports cars.

As the 1920s slipped away, lone hammers still echoed in private garages across the UK; Autocarriers Ltd changed its name to AC Ltd, and became the first British company to produce a car capable of winning the Monte Carlo Rally, which they did in 1926; the Shelby family bought their first car, a 1925 Overland tourer, son Carroll got his first ride, and Ford made plans for its first V8.

By 1932, the building of specials was becoming more refined, albeit slowly; AC Ltd had gone bankrupt, but had been saved by the Hurlock brothers, William and Charles; the Shelbys had moved to Dallas and changed the Overland for a new model, whilst son Carroll stood transfixed by his father's new car and its wire wheels; and The Ford Motor Company launched the famous flathead.

By 1950, World War II had been and gone, the sound of those hammers had risen to a crescendo, the war having armed many men with a mass of mechanical know-how. It had also caused a severe shortage of cars. John Tojeiro, an Englishman of Portuguese descent, had started work on his own special that was visually based very firmly on the Ferrari 166 Barchetta. Unbeknownst to him, Sydney Allard, John Cooper, and Colin Chapman, had also started work on projects that would put all

four of them in the history books (well, this one anyway).

The Tojeiro special's mechanics were basic. A tubular ladder frame chassis – an outrageously obvious copy of the Cooper design, but no one protested, (the Cooper family had borrowed the design from Fiat and the 500).

That's special designing for you, and subsequently, the way the Cobra came about. AC meanwhile were busy with other projects. The Hurlock brothers being engineers at heart, did not take the automotive side of their many business dealings too seriously. That is until John Tojeiro turned up at Thames Ditton having been sent to tempt the brothers in LOY 500, a special he had made for a friend. They sat up, took notice, and, being in total control of the company and therefore executive decisions, offered

They pulled out the old Lea-Francis engine, and quickly replaced it with one of their own

Then they tidied up the interior, bought it up to show standard, and launched it in 1953. Tojeiro was paid £5.00 per car

John a royalty of £5.00 per car if he would allow them to reproduce it. Thank God for small companies. Tojeiro took up the offer, and wheels started to roll.

In 1953 things started to take shape. The Earls Courts Show revealed that shape. The AC 'Ace' appeared, named after the RAC Rally winner at Monte Carlo. The appearance of a production body so close to one of their own did not seem to bother Fiat. With hindsight, and venom-covered second-place Ferraris, it may be that Fiat and their stable-mates Ferrari should have complained back then instead of licking their wounds some years later.

Left
Off to the races for an AC Ace-Bristol, which first appeared at Goodwood in 1956

Above
The beautiful AC Ace 2.6, almost identical to a Cobra – the only real exterior give-away being the lack of flared-wheel arches

Following pages
The man responsible for the Cobra, Carroll Shelby with one of his own, a racing-trim 427

But father Charles of the Cooper clan had a few words to say, once he saw 'his' chassis go from special to series production. He realised what a chance Coopers had missed. The AC show car was actually nothing more than Vin Davison's (another of John's chums) Tojeiro special that had been transformed in a matter of weeks to become the Ace. The old Lea-Francis engine had been replaced, however, by one of AC's own.

Across the Atlantic meanwhile, hints of links were starting, as Shelby, now a grown boy, had started racing. 1953 saw Shelby in his first professional race, working for Roy Cherryhomes, and behind the wheel of an American-powered British racing car, a 'Cad-engined Allard'. Shelby only lost one race that year, which is to say the least – impressive. But, more importantly, had the idea for a great Trans-Atlantic racing production car already stirred?

13

Left
A 1965 AC Cobra whose neat styling is close to the European ideal of a sports car. Owned by J H Haynes and now in the Sparkford Motor Museum

Above
GPG 4C, Charles Aggs' stunning 1964 5-litre AC Cobra in its present day red and gold paint. Note the huge rear vents

Shelby was, after all, behind the wheel of such a car almost all that year.

In 1954 the 'Ace' went into production, with several modifications, the most noticeable being the raising of those give-away 166 headlights to dramatically alter the appearance of the front end. Whilst the factory in Thames Ditton hummed with activity, Donald Healey planned his record attempt at Bonneville Salt Flats, and in the process contacted Carroll Shelby, who had his first crash at around the same time.

Although not a serious accident, he shattered his elbow, which he would remember years later when he eventually decided to quit racing. These times saw Shelby almost continually driving a Ferrari of one sort of another.

Left
John Atkins' road-look, and Martin Colvill's race-look Roadsters sitting side-by-side on the track

Above
Just to let you know his track record, John Atkins keeps a stack of scrutineers' tickets in an elastic band next to the fire-extinguisher!

Back home, and the Ace was no longer a Ferrari look-alike, it was also no longer powered by AC. In 1956 the factory dropped a 2-litre engine from the Bristol Aeroplane Company into the new car, it thus became the AC Bristol.

In its initial races, both sides of the Atlantic, the Bristol-engined AC did very well indeed. In 1957 it was entered in the 24-hours of Le Mans, and came second in its class, tenth overall, and ran at 129 mph on the Mulsanne straight. AC was on its way. Carroll meanwhile was busy crashing a Maserati at Riverside International Raceway, near Newport Beach, California – he walked away unaware that he had broken his back . . .

Two years later it was Shelby that competed at Le Mans. He, along with Roy Salvadori, drove an Aston Martin DBRI/300 to the high point of his career. He won Le Mans. Shelby also raced in both the Dutch and Portuguese Grands Prix. He and Stirling Moss then went on to win the Tourist Trophy at Goodwood, which gave them enough points to win the World Championship for their sponsors Aston Martin.

Left
The engine bay of John Atkins' 289 is a modest-looking affair, but with a 650 Holly, high lift cams, big valve GT40 heads its 100 bhp up on the original!

Right
Whereas the bay of Martin Colvill's car shouts chrome and Weber twin-choke down-drafts. Power output is around 400 bhp!

Left
Peter Voight owns 289 COB, which emerged from the factory on 23 June 1968

Above
The roll-bar is home-made and detachable, and the steering wheel with its assymetric design distinguishes the Mk II from the Mk I

A year after that, while still winning races, Shelby had to reconsider the course his life was taking. He had won the Riverside Grand Prix driving a 4.5-litre Tipo 61 Birdcage Maserati; but his doctor diagnosed Angina Pectoralis as the reason for the pains in his chest that had been bothering him for years. Shelby decided to quit racing, aged 37, but won the United States Automobile Club (USAC)-championship before retiring.

Much of Shelby's racing career had had strong connections with Riverside. It was where he ran his last race, but it would be a place where, in later years, he would return to share greater triumphs. But instead of being the guy behind the wheel, he would be the guy behind the car.

In an interview at the time, Shelby said "After you get skinned and cut up enough, you begin to look around for another kind of business". Although the angina was the main reason for his retirement, he never forgot the few crashes he had suffered, especially his broken back. Although plans brewed in his head for the production of the ultimate sports car, the 'fastest in the world', his next immediate job was Western Distributor for Goodyear racing tyres.

This was followed fairly rapidly in 1961 with the opening of the Shelby School of High Performance Driving, located, of course, in Riverside. Again it appears as if the job was a 'time-killer', with Shelby's mind racing in other directions – the ultimate sports car. Dean Moon, one of the all-time automotive greats, having offered up a nice little speed shop to Shelby and his often unrecognised contemporary Peter Brock, paved the way for the beginning of the project. Brock had worked on the Sting Ray project for General Motors, and was an extremely talented young stylist and designer; but in common with Shelby he did not agree with the way big corporations worked.

Back in the UK, Ken Russell, an avid special builder, had had a notable amount of success stuffing over-weight British Ford Zephyr engines into many AC chassis. Also the Bristol Aeroplane Company had ceased building automobile engines for such cars as Frazer-Nash, Arnholt-Bristol, but more importantly, the AC Car Company. In fact, both events were so notable that the news travelled over the Atlantic, across America to the West Coast, and was told to a man in a bar named Carroll Shelby.

Side-on, and the unflared rear arches show clearly how beautiful the car was originally. Many 289s have been flared to accommodate bigger tyres

APA 6B was the second right hand drive
Cobra, and was used as a factory
demonstrator. Originally green it has
since been painted Lancia-maroon

The Story Hots Up

The letter sent to the Hurlock brothers in Thames Ditton arrived on 8 September 1961. It mentioned no specifics, just that a Texan of considerable driving ability (amongst other talents) wanted to use a car body AC produced, and to drop a big fat American V8 into it. No mention of Ford was made, just a big American V8, for at the time, Shelby had other ideas, including a Chevy block, rum-

Left
76 COB, restored as are many British Cobras, by Brian Angliss. It first saw the open road in 1966. Unlike almost all the others, it's still the original colour

Below
It is one of the small wheel-arched 7-litre beasts, and sports the correct Halibrand wheels, and exact-replica side-pipes

Left
*Face-to-face with the children. Mum
and Dad Roadsters look on as a
handful of Shelby GT350 Mustangs
stare back*

Above
*GTM 700F is a full-race bodied 427
with an impressive record of 10 firsts
and 5 second places out of 16 starts*

bling in his head. Chevrolet was actually approached, but said,
'No thanks – why create competition for the Corvette?'

At the time he made contact with AC, Shelby was unaware of
Ford Motor Company's (FoMoCo) new casting technique that produced a lightweight, thin-wall, cast-iron engine block. It was
planned for use in the Fairlane. When he heard the news, he
mailed another letter, this time to Ford. AC had already replied
with enthusiasm. Dave Evans, in charge of Ford's stock car racing
programme, called up and said 'Yes, we'll give you two engines –
free!' Things were starting to shift.

On different sides of the Atlantic the Hurlocks and Shelby (not
forgetting Brock) worked on alterations to the chassis in order to
accommodate the bigger engine. By November 1961 FoMoCo's
engines had arrived at Dean Moon's workshop, where he proved
invaluable with the race tuning and development process. Next,

A 1971 AC 428 fastback. The lines, by Frua, were definitely designed for the European market

Dave Evans telephoned with news that Ford had now developed a high performance version of the lightweight engine. It would be 260 cubic inches and, yet again, Ford were willing to donate two engines to the project.

Meanwhile, AC negotiations were going well. The first V8 had arrived in the UK just before the year ended. William Hurlock fondly remembers the occasion. When the first engine was delivered, one of his employees relayed the event, but was a little confused at the lack of paper work that had come with it. All he could do was take a helpful guess, and tell Mr Hurlock that he thought the engine must have come from Japan, for it bore the inscription 'FoMoCo'.

But the name confused some, for although the 7-litre engine gave 345 bhp, it was obviously a lot less powerful than the 427

January 1962 saw Shelby on a plane destined for the UK, and a quick test drive. A prototype was, with the exception of a few nuts and bolts, ready. The first V8 had, as we know, already arrived, and Shelby, having apparently given the car a quick spin around Silverstone where he had time to test its top-end on the straights, its stopping ability, and handling features (fast, jolting, and vice-like) returned home.

Before the first car docked in the Port of Los Angeles, Shelby reputedly had a dream in which he saw the name Cobra on the front of a car. Apparently in the morning he realised this should be the name of the car that realised his dream. Confused!? Peter Brock loved the idea, and had a logo designed straight away.

There was a slight hitch when they discovered that the name was already being used by Crossley to designate their engines that were fabricated using copper as a brazing medium – C0pper BRAzing. This naming difficulty was soon overcome.

By the time the body arrived in the United States, there were few alterations left to be made (although the Americans would have liked to think otherwise). Almost all necessary modifications had already taken place. The front end of the first Shelby car was exactly the same as the AC Ace 2.6, with the exception of the steering box position, which was canted to allow room for the wider V8 engine. The chassis needed a whole new rear end carrier assembly to cope with the increased torque. Shelby specified inboard disc-brakes, although AC were wary. All future Cobras resorted to outboard 'anchors'.

There is an argument that is still debated, concerning the chassis designation of this first Stateside car, and what it stood for. The three prefix letters were definitely CSX. What is in dispute, is what the 'X' stood for. Generally the Stateside team insist it stood for X-perimental, whereas the UK team contest it stood for X-port, and seeing as they are the ones that kept the books, and designated chassis numbers, and that 'X' had always stood for X-port in the past, I can see no reason for them to have changed their ways, which had, incidentally, remained almost the same for 60 years. It seems more likely that the Stateside team wished for the Cobra to become, as quickly as possible, a product of the US, not UK, nor even a combination of the two. This may be why many americans came to call the car 'British-bodied', implying that the shells were simply sent from the UK, and Shelby had done the rest. What actually happened in Britain, as we know, was a lot more than just that. Anyway, as far as I'm concerned, it was irrelevant then, and it's irrelevant now. More importantly, the first Cobra had arrived.

Back to the story, and we join CSX 2000 (or 0001) at Moon's shop, where he assisted Shelby and Brock on cramming in the lightweight engine that had arrived from Ford in the meantime. At some point CSX was taken to Dearborn, Michigan, where it was shown-off to Don Frey, (a senior Ford executive) who agreed

What can I say? It's bright isn't it?

Left
The immaculate 427 COB, as owned by John Stevens, was given to AC Cars, who took a year to complete this fault-less restoration

Above
Re-imported to the UK in 1973, the car is not raced, but just sits pretty between runs

Left
Dick Smith behind the wheel of his 427 in a Californian Hill Climb

Above
GD 100, a 289 Sports built in 1966, displays the novice cross to warn other racers to take care

to supply engines on credit for future enterprises. What he apparently said was 'I think we may have something here'. Luckily for Shelby, Frey, along with making vast under-statements, was a sports car enthusiast. He knew all about the Texan, and his racing exploits. Had it not been for Frey's genuinely rare enthusiasm for sports cars, and subsequent slight bias, the AC Cobra might never had shed its first skin.

At the New York Automobile Show in April 1962 Shelby was a guest on the Ford stand. This invitation was a result of a meeting with Evans in California, where he experienced the car, and all its deadly potential. Ford's backing and involvement was imperative, otherwise their car would be simply another hot rod. To ensure that the car got noticed amongst all the other exhibits, Shelby had paint-wizard Dean Jeffreys, create a 'noticeable' paint colour. It was almost omni-present, a yellow pearlescent paint that, under

Above
Just for looks, rear wing air-vents did not appear on any Roadsters, although they were used on the King Cobra

Right
This high-performance 289 has dispensed with the troublesome Ford Autolite carb that was used on the original Fairlane derived engine

the electric lighting, seemed to shine like the sun. The car, of course, stormed the show. The Cobra was poised, and ready to strike.

August 1962, four months after the New York Automobile Show, Ford hammered out a deal with Shelby which included buying facilities near Venice Beach, Los Angeles, at 1042 Princeton Drive. Vacated by the bankcrupt Woolworth heir Lance Reventlow, the complex was purpose built for building Reventlow's Scarab racing cars. Phil Remington, one of the most talented Mechanics (note the capitals) at the time, came with the walls. 'If Phil Remington's a Mechanic, then at least 99 per cent of the others who carry that title are imposters', said Shelby. It was Remington that prepared the first Cobras for racing.

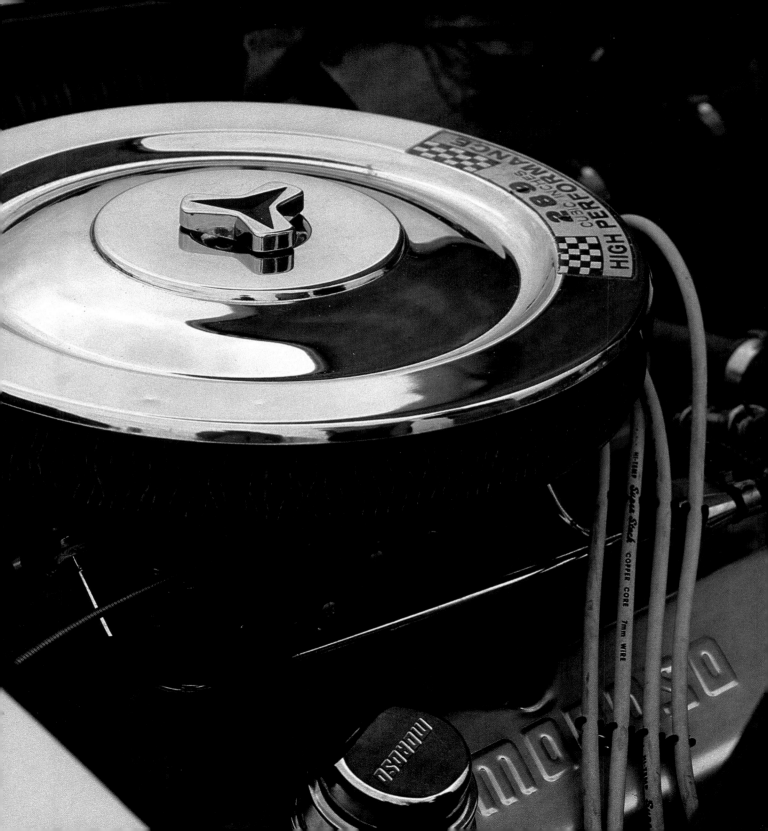

Left
This pristine racing bodied 427 is ready and waiting, three spare 'cold-air' boxes that separated the carbs from the engine sit out in front

Above
A 289 Cobra taking the bend in the 1965 Le Mans, which saw 11 Ford powered cars take on 12 Ferraris

Above
John Atkins behind the wheel of his famous 1965 Mark II Cobra which has been de-screened for the race

Left
Feel like a blast?

Above
*427s, 289s, and Coupés deceptively
dormant*

Right
*A much meaner 427 plus its strong-
armed driver taking a corner at
Silverstone*

Above
A beautiful shot of the 289

Following pages
39PH with its aluminium roof in place. Streamlined to improve speeds down the Mulsanne Straight at Le Mans, the filler cap was, due to the necessary boot re-design, located in the roof

Left
Two racing-bodied 427s battle round corners in the Bahamian sunshine

A 427 and 289 battle it out in the Bahamas . . .

. . . as the 289 takes the lead . . .

the 427 roars after him . . .

. . . and nearly achieves lift-off as it hurtles into the corner

Above
GTM 700F sits with another member of
team, the roaring Mk III GT40, one of
the seven built by Ford Advanced
Vehicles in Slough. Note through the
Roadsters screen the front wing oil-filler

Right
The beautiful Daytona Coupé as
designed by Peter Brock. Note the
recessed fuel-filler

Above
The Shelby American team colours were viking-blue and yellow

Above left
Another Englishman abroad, this time it's the 1965 Spa 1000 km

Below left
This semi-race 5-litre Cobra debuted at the 1964 British GP. It is seen more commonly in this book in its present colours of red and gold

Above

John Atkins streaks past on his way to another victory

Above left

Dan Gurney in the seat at the 1965 Le Mans in this Cobra Coupé

Below left

A quick chat before 39 PH, ex-member of the Willment racing team, blasts back onto the tarmac to clock up some more competition mileage

Above
Silverstone 1985, and the Post Historic Sports Car Club plays host to its victor of 1982 and 1983, John Aitkins and his Mark II

Above left
Out on the blistering black-top this State-side Cobra would probably pass the fried-egg test!

Below left
Rounding the corner at Druids Bend, Brands Hatch, is another John Atkins Roadster

Above
The Daytona Coupé with its aero-dynamic styling which included faired-in headlights à la E-type

Right
The Daytona's curved Plexiglass windows did not help the aerodynamics, but they stopped the driver roasting

Above
676 COB, a racing bodied Cobra, plus aluminium hard-top clearly displays its Ferrari-influenced egg-crate grille

Above Right
A side-piped Roadster blasts past, much happier on arid American asphalt than the slippery surfaces of an English meeting

Below Right
A 289 experiencing a little pitch and yaw as its sails around a corner in another Post Historic Championship

This 289 left Thames Ditton in 1966, already fitted with a Holley carb amongst other performance boosters. It is still winning races

Above
The Willment Cobra Coupé at Brands Hatch in 1983. Note the air-duct mid-bonnet

Right
The Coupé's flip-front made engine access easy and fast. The radiator was enclosed and ducts allowed the hot-air to escape

Another Cobra, another race . . .

Above
*Stateside again, and the driver
concentrates on race tactics, whilst
never forgetting to be wary of the side-
pipes on exit*

Right
*The Silverstone circuit plays host to
another 289, this time it's 1987*

Racing Cobras and the New Breed

Proving yourself in motor racing circles is above all about proving your product. Kipling may have had a lot to say that was wise about the motives and emotions of winning – 'If you can meet with triumph and disaster and treat those two imposters just the same . . ', but, if we face the grim facts, everybody wants to win. Especially when the game is commercial, then to win becomes imperative. There was no other reason why Shelby was so keen that his Cobras go racing. Do not disillusion yourself, competition is rarely the spirit of adventure. Shelby's idea was quite simple: win the Sport Car Club of America (SCCA) Class A Production Championship, along with the US Road Racing Championship, and finally, win the World Manufacturers Championship, and you enjoy all the glory and the profits.

October 1962 saw the second Cobra, CSX 2002, now converted for competition, on its first outing. Billy Krause drove it in the 'Experimental Production Class' at Riverside. Having stormed ahead of a field of Corvettes, a rear-hub carrier broke, and the Cobra DNF'd (Did Not Finish). It was not important. Reliability could be worked on and improved, but the car's brute power had been noted by all. Phil Remington set to work on a new set of hub carriers, finished the next day, and Shelby American was back in business.

Billy Krause was again behind the wheel of CSX 2000 in its second race, at Nassau, upper New York state. Now Nassau Speed Week is a bit of a strange affair, it's really a promotional week for the Nassau Hotel Association, who provide free everything for those that attend. Probably the only reason so many leading manufacturers turn up is the extremely rough course. It was a good test of Shelby's new car – the theory being that if it did not break or fall off at Nassau, it would not fail anywhere. Were it not for a bolt coming loose, the Cobra would almost definitely

The rear-end of the Daytona is as unmistakable as it is stunning. Note the vents

Above
*Brighton Speed Trials has always proved
popular with Cobras – probably because
no corners are involved*

Right
*The 289 seems to be having as many
problems, if not more*

have won. As it was, the errant bolt led to the change over to rack and pinion steering.

But the Nassau Week was not over, the 3-hour Trophy Race was still to be run. Krause again behind the wheel, and halfway through, with nothing going wrong, Krause pulled into the pits, and Shelby re-filled the twin tanks. He shouted 'That's enough!', and Krause roared off, still way ahead, until that is, he ran out of petrol. Shelby, much to his embarrassment, had forgotten to let the fuel drain through the first tank and into the second.

Modifications were obviously carried out on CSX 2002 and subsequent racing Cobras to prepare them for competition. These alterations were quite permissible in sports car racing, and they were not just for speed. Most also increased safety. Oil coolers were installed, along with larger capacity sumps, and a heavy duty

A confident owner leaves his 427 open to inspection

Out in the Nevada sunshine, this 427, a guest at a Ferrari Hill Climb went on (much to the F.O.C.'s disgust) to take Fastest Time of the Day

clutch. Shock absorbers were usually left as standard Konis, but with stiffer settings.

The engines received the usual balancing and polishing, with modifications allowed to the valves, cylinders, heads, camshafts etc. Carburettor jet alterations were allowed, something which Shelby quickly capitalised upon. In the States, Plexiglass windscreens replaced the heavier standard glass ones, but the **FIA**, Federation International de l'Automobile, did not permit this in Europe, where only 5 per cent of a car's homologated weight could be lost by the removal of peripheral items such as wipers and carpets.

Gearboxes and final drive ratios could, of course, be altered to suit specific circuits. Double-capacity brake fluid reservoirs ensured that were there to be a hydraulics problem, the car could

still slow down satisfactorily. Also a 37-gallon fuel tank replaced the standard 14-gallon unit, and huge racing exhausts were provided by Derrington in the UK. Shelby was astute enough to realise that some customers would want to race the cars themselves. So by 1964 he was offering four versions of the 289 Cobra. Standard; a bit better than Standard; a bit better still; or a replica Shelby FIA team car, as tested by Ken Miles (or so they said) and purchasable for an arm and a leg.

Back to the story, and a new year, 1963. The Cobra was lying, waiting to strike. A new team member, Dave MacDonald had the pleasure of taking the AC to its first victory. The setting was Riverside – Shelby had returned for the first of those triumphs. Ken Miles, a British driver, was MacDonald's team-mate, and he

Above
John Atkins at the tail-fins of a Tiger, which just missed the photographer's toes

Right
This 289 sits under the US sky just waiting to get out on the track and spit venom at that Porsche

actually had the audacity to pit-stop half-way through the race – for a drink of water. He went on to re-overtake the whole field, and take second place behind MacDonald.

I shall not bother to go into details of its next race, the Daytona Continental, suffice to say that the Cobra's suffered teething problems, and Ferraris took first, second and third.

In their first full year of racing two Cobras entered the 24-heures du Mans, the infamous endurance race. The course is in excess of 2700 miles, with a lap of 8.3 miles. One team was sponsored by *The Sunday Times*, and entered by AC with Stirling Moss as boss; and the other was a private Stateside entry. Both Cobras were capable of hitting 165 mph on the three-mile Mulsanne straight, but the results were poor. The US entry DNF'd, and the AC sponsored Cobra ended up 7th behind six Ferraris. Who ever said the Cobra won everything?

At the National SCCA meet at Lake Garnett, Kansas, 7 July 1963, it was real Cobra versus Corvette stuff, and the first real victory. Cobras took 1st, 2nd and 3rd to the Corvettes' 4th, 5th and 6th. Enough said.

Above
The Bell and Colvill Cobra, more commonly seen flashing past in the hands of Martin Colvill, is a much developed Mark II

Right
The Daytona GT of 1966 saw Roadsters battling with Ferraris on the banking, even though Shelby had stopped racing them at the end of 1965

A trio of Roadsters and a pair of Shelby's new King Cobras arrived for Nassau that year. The King Cobra was just a British Cooper Monaco chassis (note the Cooper clan did finally get in on the act) that Shelby had stuffed another Ford V8 into. This time there was no backing from Ford, who were busy working on the GT40 project. The press named them King Cobras, but they should really have been known as Cooper-Cobras. What the team were unaware of was the bite-back Chevrolet had in store, having just received an injection of private money. Basically, the Cobra team were not bitten, they were slaughtered.

Throughout the following season of 1964, four Daytona coupés and four 289 Roadsters were used in competition. The 289s were referred to as FIA Roadsters as they were built specifically for FIA regulations.

On the 16 February the barely finished Peter Brock-designed coupé with its streamlined body and strengthened chassis raced for the first time, at the Daytona International Speedway. It did not have a name before the race, the car had only been conceived in October the previous year, (Brock and Miles spent a busy winter) so people referred to it as 'the Daytona Coupé'. It stuck. Throughout most of the race they were in the lead, but at the last pit stop the new edition to the Cobra family burst into flames. It managed to regain some credit for setting the fastest lap time, which took a little of the glory away from the triumphant Ferraris.

The Sebring 12-hour race at the International Raceway in Florida, was in March, and a set of four 289 Roadsters, plus a Coupé or two, were competing alongside a Ken Miles built 'hot-rod' – the first big-engined Cobra. A Mark II fitted with a 427 engine, the handling of said car apparently being compared by both drivers to a '48 Buick! In fact, the handling was so bad that in practice Miles hit a tree, and the car was withdrawn from the race, much to the relief of other competitors. The coupé took 1st in the GT classification, but 4th overall, beaten out of the top three by a batch of prototype Ferraris. The Roadsters held their own, and took most of the top places in the GT class.

The Daytona Coupé, which took its name from the race, comes out of Druids, the nasty hair-pin at Brands that has caused many a head to spin

Above
This exhaustive detail of a 289 gently hints that seeing the back-end of a Cobra at such close range is not a usual occurrence

Left
Taking corners is, as you may have noticed, a hairy and very physical task if you are behind the wheel of a Cobra

Ford's GT40 made its debut on 13 May at the Nurburgring. The Ring proved no place for the coupé, and the Roadsters did not do well either, with none of the team finishing in a decent position. At least the rather unexciting first race outing of the GT40 (it was not a brilliant performer that day) took some attention away from the Cobras' embarrassing trot around the course.

Three Daytona Coupés entered in the 24-hours of Le Mans in 1964, two of them Shelby backed. With oil temperatures rising to over 300°C, one still managed to win its GT class, with the other DFN-ing. The other Daytona Coupé, AC backed, failed to finish after a rear tyre blow-out. It was just as well no Roadsters were entered that year. The coupés had been prepared in double-quick time, and with a Roaster present it may well be that the scrutineers would have noticed, by comparison, one or two discrepancies in the chassis and frame structure of the Daytona!

But what really caught everyone's attention at Le Mans that year was the GT40s first real race. Their appearance caused confusion as both they and the Cobras ran in viking blue colours. Phil Remington's habit of hopping from car to car, driving whatever he fancied at the time, did not help matters either. The GT40s were actually with the Cobra team, but just good friends as opposed to family.

The RAC Tourist Trophy at Goodwood saw the World Championship points gap between Ferrari and Cobra narrow to eleven. Shelby American had to win two out of the three remaining races – the *Coppa d'Europa* at Monza, the *Tour de France*, and the Double 500 at Long Island (all set to take place that September) to claim the Championship.

Carroll was counting on the *Coppa d'Europa*, and the Double 500, as their chances in the *Tour de France* were almost nil. Now, the *Coppa d'Europa* in Italy is basically Ferrari's 'own' turf. They were not prepared to lose to some dust-kicking chicken farmer from Texas. So the ever proud and patriotic Italians came up with an answer. They insisted that the 250LM and 275LM Ferraris be FIA homologated as GT cars so they could enter the race.

If for any reason this was not acceptable (like past dubious homologations – the original GTO with less than 100 in existence) then they would, for the sake of the nation's pride, have to call the race off. The FIA refused their deal. There were only about 10 LMs then built. The organisers at Monza, on hearing the decision, cancelled the race, and took with it, co-incidentally of course,

Shelby's hopes of winning the Championship for 1964.

So, the end of a year which did not fulfill the Cobra dream. What would 1965 bring? Would the Daytonas keep pace with the GT40, or was the writing on the wall? And what about the Italians, they obviously were not taking Kipling's words to heart. They wanted to win, and, it seemed, that if they could not, then nobody would. What would 1965 bring? The FIA World Championship?

Certainly the challenge of the Corvette had gone. It had felt the lash of the Cobra, and been beaten. So badly beaten in fact, that by the beginning of 1965 one of Shelby's biggest distributors had sniffed out all the local Corvette owners, and sent them a snake-bite kit! Just for promotional purposes you must understand.

One of the first major happenings of the year was from Detroit. Ford, frustrated with the GT40, and its poor reliability record, handed the project over to Shelby. It came with money, and a good deal of media coverage – Shelby was not likely to say no. The battle for homologation started early, with both Ferrari and Shelby fighting for that vital GT classification. Shelby was in the blue corner rooting for the 427, and Ferrari in the rosso, probably even seeing red, was still fighting tooth and nail for the 250LM.

The FIA stood their ground, and who could blame them? With previous Ferrari behaviour in mind, they came to their decision. Neither the 427 nor the 250LM would be homologated as GT cars. Enzo was furious. He resigned from the Automobile Club of Italy, and thus the FIA. He therefore left the World Championship open to privately entered Ferraris, or more likely, Shelby American, the Daytona Coupés, and the GT40s.

The six Coupés raced in 1964 were given a really thorough re-working, and by the beginning of the 1965 season, they were ready and waiting for the green light.

The Daytona won its GT class at its namesake track in the Continental 2000 km, 28 February 1965. Tactics had been simple. The Daytonas put pressure on Ferraris, the GT40s held back, and they all charged for the final run. It worked, with a GT40 first; a

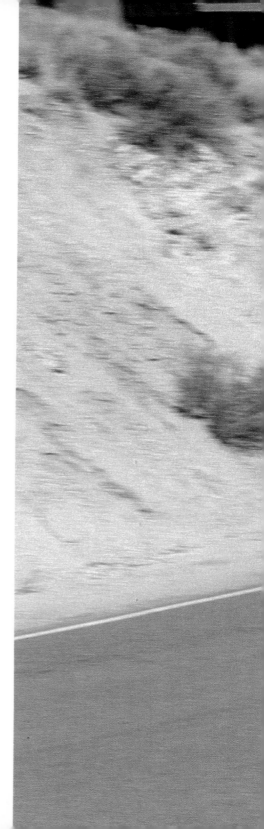

Dick Smith owns and races this 427, and when a Porsche 930 Turbo matched his time-record at this US hill-climb, he went out and set a new one!

Coupé 2nd; a GT40 3rd; and Coupé 4th! They had shut the door without even giving the Ferraris a chance to hit open air.

A month later at Sebring, the Shelby team appeared with two GT40s and four Daytona Coupés. An unpleasant sight for any Ferrari competitor. The outrageous rainfall (so heavy that alloy wheels with inflated tyres were actually seen floating around the pits) did not harm the Daytonas. They miraculously kept going to take 1/3/2/ and 4th place in the GT class.

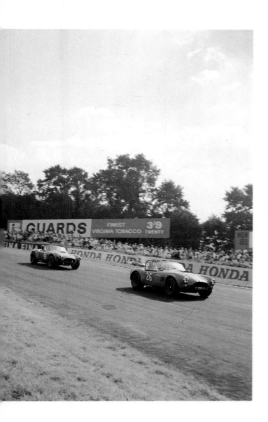

Left
The Bell and Colvill 289 head on and ready to race

Above
Cobras thunder through the straight during 1964 Brands Hatch meeting. Notice red car which has come on terms with advertising hoarding

Allan Mann Racing, the competition arm of Ford's biggest British distributor, received a twin-set of two GT40s and two Coupés to prepare for the first European battle of the year, the Monza 1000 km in April.

Enzo had decided to allow his prototypes to start competing again, obviously realising that that dust-kicker from Texas was going to walk the Championship if he did not do something about it, pronto! Thus the GT40 was up against the stiff opposition of Ferraris new 4-litre P2s. The Daytonas on the other hand, being in 'Enzos last stand' GT class, did not have much to watch out for in their rear-view mirrors. What they did have was the *Curva Parabollica*, a 180 degree bend – it's what Monza is most famous for. Luckily the Daytonas, unlike the GT40s, were used to a rough ride. They had been built at about the same time as the track, and they handled the corners perfectly. They came 1st and 2nd in class, 8th and 9th overall.

The Nurburgring race, 23 May, was approached with caution. Three Coupés, all of which had never run on anything but Goodyear rubber, were suddenly, after a day of testing, running on Firestones. They won – 1/2/3 in class. The GT40s, on the other hand, seem to relive the failures of the Cobras a year earlier, with four of them starting out, and only one finishing.

Le Mans came around again, with five Daytonas, four GT40s, and two new 427 Mark Is. Six hours into the race, and all the GT40s and 427s had dropped out. With four of the Daytonas DNFing, that left one remaining Coupé to take a lonely second in class.

By the time Allan Mann had prepared two Daytonas for the 12-hourer at Rheims on 4 July, it was a dead cert that they would win the Manufacturers' Championship. Bondurant and Schlesser won the GT class, with Sear and Whitmore close on their heels, which was good enough to win them the World Manufacturers' Championship. Shelby had realised his dream. On the racing circuit at least, there was nothing left to do.

The AC Cobra Mark IV photographed outside its home on the Brooklands banking. Brian Angliss of Autokraft has finally managed to gain rights to manufacture these brand new Cobras. This is no kit. The bulbous shape is almost identical to the Cobra Mk III, one of the only exterior differences is the Mk IV's lack of two extra frontal intake grilles

Above and Right
The quality of the Autokraft Mk IV Cobra is seen in every angle and every detail

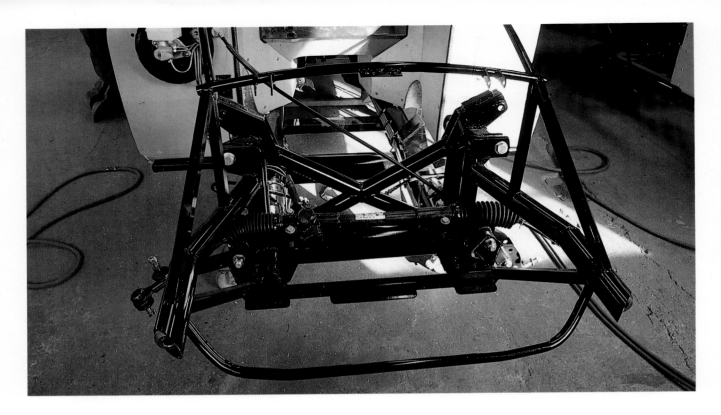

Above
The main chassis is constructed from 4-inch diameter cold drawn steel tubing

Above right
The original jig used on the 427 is still used, and it's all MIG welded for minimum distortion . . .

Below right
. . . although many improvements have been made so the Mk IV complies with current Impact Safety regulations

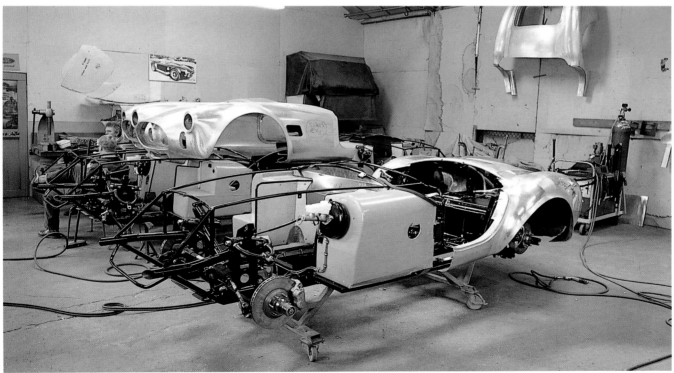

Above
Few cars are still hand-built, the Mk IV is one of them

Right
The one-piece footbox/bulkhead unit and integral wheel arch panelling is moulded in GRP

Left
It takes 200-man hours to construct a bodyshell . . .

Above
. . . using age-old techniques on the 16-gauge aluminium sheet

Above
Front and rears line up, waiting to join the chassis

Right
The meaty V8 that says it all. Well, 'Get out of my way' at least!

Above
Once the perfected bodyshell is in one piece . . .

Above left
Autokraft also undertake numerous other projects, one of the more common is work on older Cobras

Below left
Such work usually involves a total ground-up restoration. Almost all the concours Cobras on British roads have been repaired here

Following pages
It's off to the spray booth. The shell is lightly coated in filler to even out any miniscule defects – which is a lot better than the originals, they were daubed with 5 thick coats of the same material

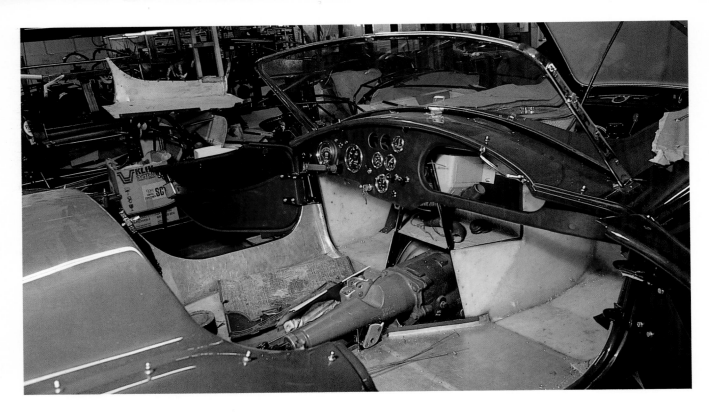

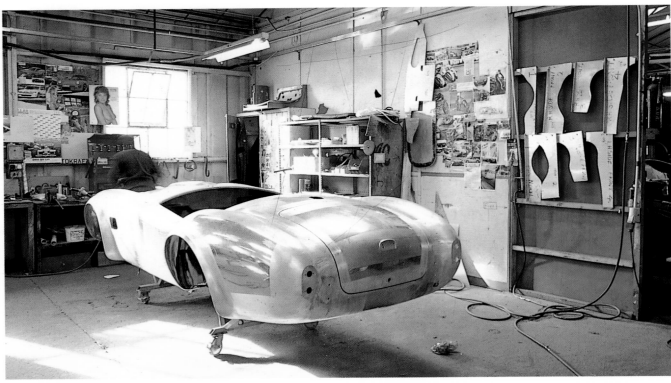

Above
Discs all around

Above left
Once the 14-layer painting process has finished, it's on with the chrome

Below left
The skilled workmen employed to build these beautiful cars are almost as rare as the cars

Above
Everything is almost ready. Final checks are made . . .

Right
. . . close-up!

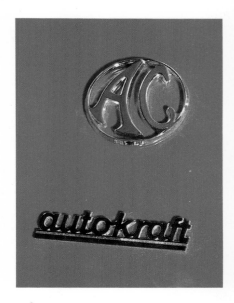

Above
Then some poor soul has to take a steady hand, and drill in the holes for the badge. Badge in place, a quick re-polish, and the car's ready for the road

Right
After the AC 289, and the 428, AC were experiencing financial difficulties. They came up with the AC 3000ME (3-litre Mid-engined), it was similar to the Fiat XI/9, and unveiled in 1972

Above
*If you thought that was bad, then the
1979 version was an even more sorry
sight. Quite revolting in fact*

Previous pages
*The 1977 Ford Mustang Cobra II, a car
far removed from the original Cobra. It
did not deserve to sport the Cobra
name*

Right
*The Ghia 3000ME was a much more
acceptable looking car, it was first seen
at the 1981 Geneva Motor Show*

*Owned by Ford, the Ghia 3000ME
sadly never made it into production*

Above
The Ghia Cobra prototype of 1965 did not get much further either. Getting confused?

Right
The Cobra 230 ME was a promising prototype that got no further than that. Mid-engined yet again, it bore more than a passing resemblance to the RS200

Above
Even for a courtesy run on an enclosed track crash helmets are mandatory

Above left
On the Members' Banking at Brooklands a Cobra looks back along the world's first purpose built motor sport circuit. The track, although it was the scene of many record breaking successes it was deemed unsafe for cars with the speed of a Cobra and consequently lapsed

Below left
Frayed carpet on the transmission tunnel and well-worn trim reveal that this Cobra was, and is, driven hard. Only the foolish claim they ever tame the car. It demands respect at all times

Left
It may be overcast, but it is hot out there on this raceway in the deep South. Notice the sophisticated control tower. The white car with the bandaged nose is about to be lapped by the Cobra

Above
Cobra cars and drivers are a race apart. Almost universally they prefer sober, no-nonsense colours to the over-sponsored warpaint common with other marques

Above
Many USA registered Cobras have 'vanity' plates which have variations on the 'Snake' and 'Cobra' theme

Right
A thing of unsurpassable automotive beauty

The badge – for those who have the
courage